THOMAS CRANE PUBLIC LIBRARY
QUINCY MASS
CITY APPROPRIATION

AMERICANS MOVE WEST
(1846-1860)

HOW AMERICA BECAME AMERICA

TITLE LIST

THE NORTHERN COLONIES: Freedom to Worship (1600-1770)

THE SOUTHERN COLONIES: The Search for Wealth (1600-1770)

AMERICA IS BORN (1770-1800)

THOMAS JEFFERSON AND THE GROWING UNITED STATES (1800-1811)

WARS AT HOME: America Forms an Identity (1812-1820)

REMEMBER THE ALAMO: Americans Fight for Texas (1820-1845)

AMERICANS MOVE WEST (1846-1860)

THE CIVIL WAR: America Torn Apart (1860-1865)

AMERICAN WILDERNESS: Alaska and the National Parks (1865-1890)

BEYOND OUR SHORES: America Extends Its Reach (1890-1899)

A SHIFTING ROLE: America and the World (1900-1912)

AMERICA IN THE 20TH CENTURY (1913-1999)

CONNECTING THE 21ST CENTURY TO THE PAST: What Makes America America? (2000-the present)

HOW AMERICA BECAME AMERICA

AMERICANS MOVE WEST
(1846-1860)

BY TERESA LACLAIR

MASON CREST

Mason Crest
370 Reed Road
Broomall, Pennsylvania 19008
www.masoncrest.com

Copyright © 2013 by Mason Crest, an imprint of National Highlights, Inc. All rights reserved. No part of this publication may be reproduced or transmitted in any form or by any means, electronic or mechanical, including photocopying, recording, taping, or any information storage and retrieval system, without permission from the publisher.

Printed and bound in Hashemite Kingdom of Jordan.

First printing
9 8 7 6 5 4 3 2 1

Library of Congress Cataloging-in-Publication Data

LaClair, Teresa.
 Americans move West (1846-1860) / Teresa LaClair.
     p. cm. — (How America became America)
 Includes bibliographical references and index.
  ISBN 978-1-4222-2403-8 (hardcover) — ISBN 978-1-4222-2396-3 (hardcover series) — ISBN 978-1-4222-9313-3 (ebook)
 1. West (U.S.)—History—1848-1860—Juvenile literature. 2. Overland journeys to the Pacific—Juvenile literature. I. Title.
 F593.L17 2013
 978'.02—dc23
                              2012012040

Produced by Harding House Publishing Services, Inc.
www.hardinghousepages.com
Cover design by Torque Advertising + Design.

CONTENTS

Time Line   6
1. Manifest Destiny   9
2. War with Mexico   17
3. Why People Moved West   25
4. Life on the Oregon Trail   33
5. A Railroad Across the United States   39
Find Out More   46
Index   47
About the Author and the Consultant   48

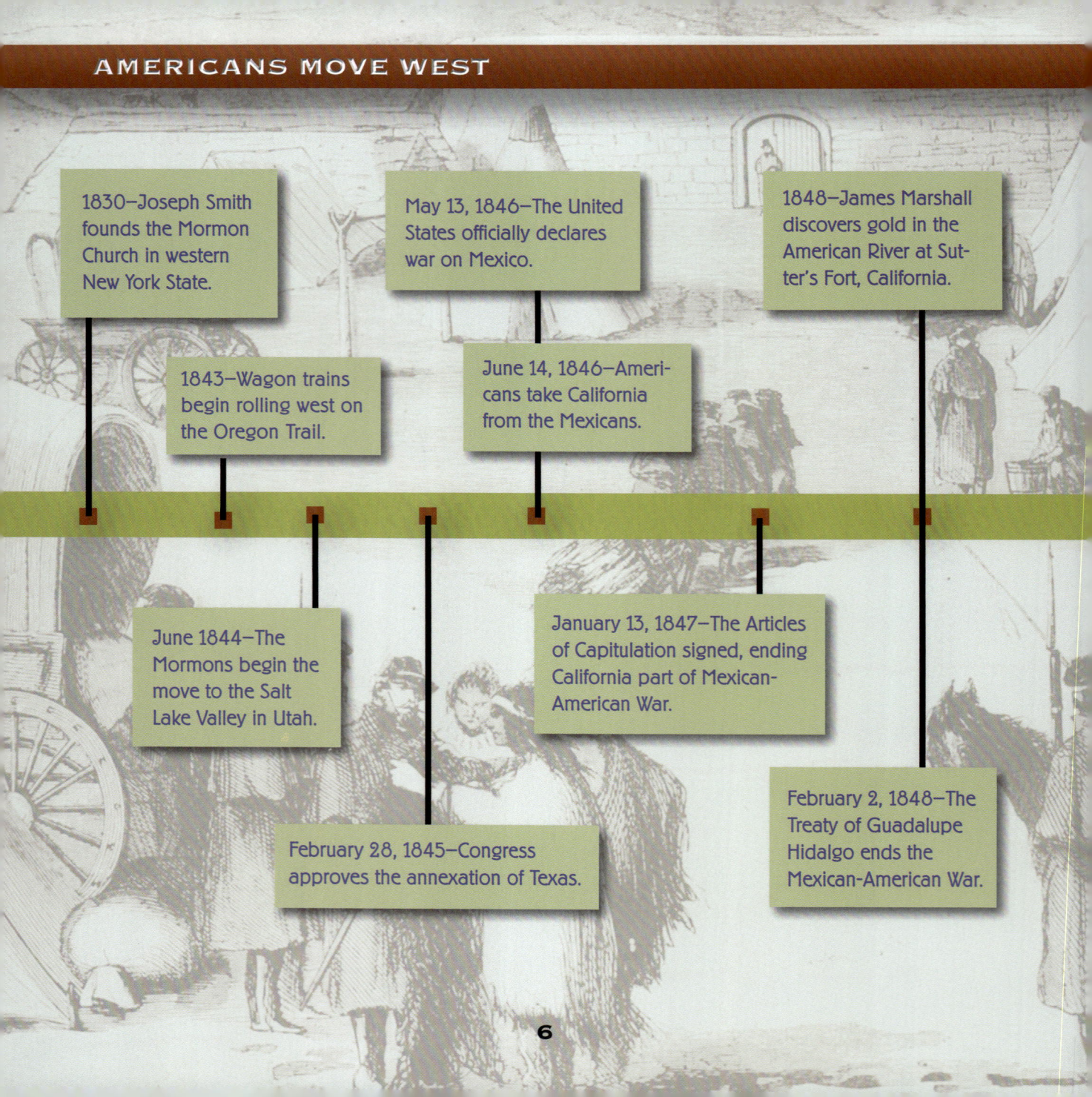

AMERICANS MOVE WEST

1830—Joseph Smith founds the Mormon Church in western New York State.

1843—Wagon trains begin rolling west on the Oregon Trail.

June 1844—The Mormons begin the move to the Salt Lake Valley in Utah.

February 28, 1845—Congress approves the annexation of Texas.

May 13, 1846—The United States officially declares war on Mexico.

June 14, 1846—Americans take California from the Mexicans.

January 13, 1847—The Articles of Capitulation signed, ending California part of Mexican-American War.

1848—James Marshall discovers gold in the American River at Sutter's Fort, California.

February 2, 1848—The Treaty of Guadalupe Hidalgo ends the Mexican-American War.

Time Line

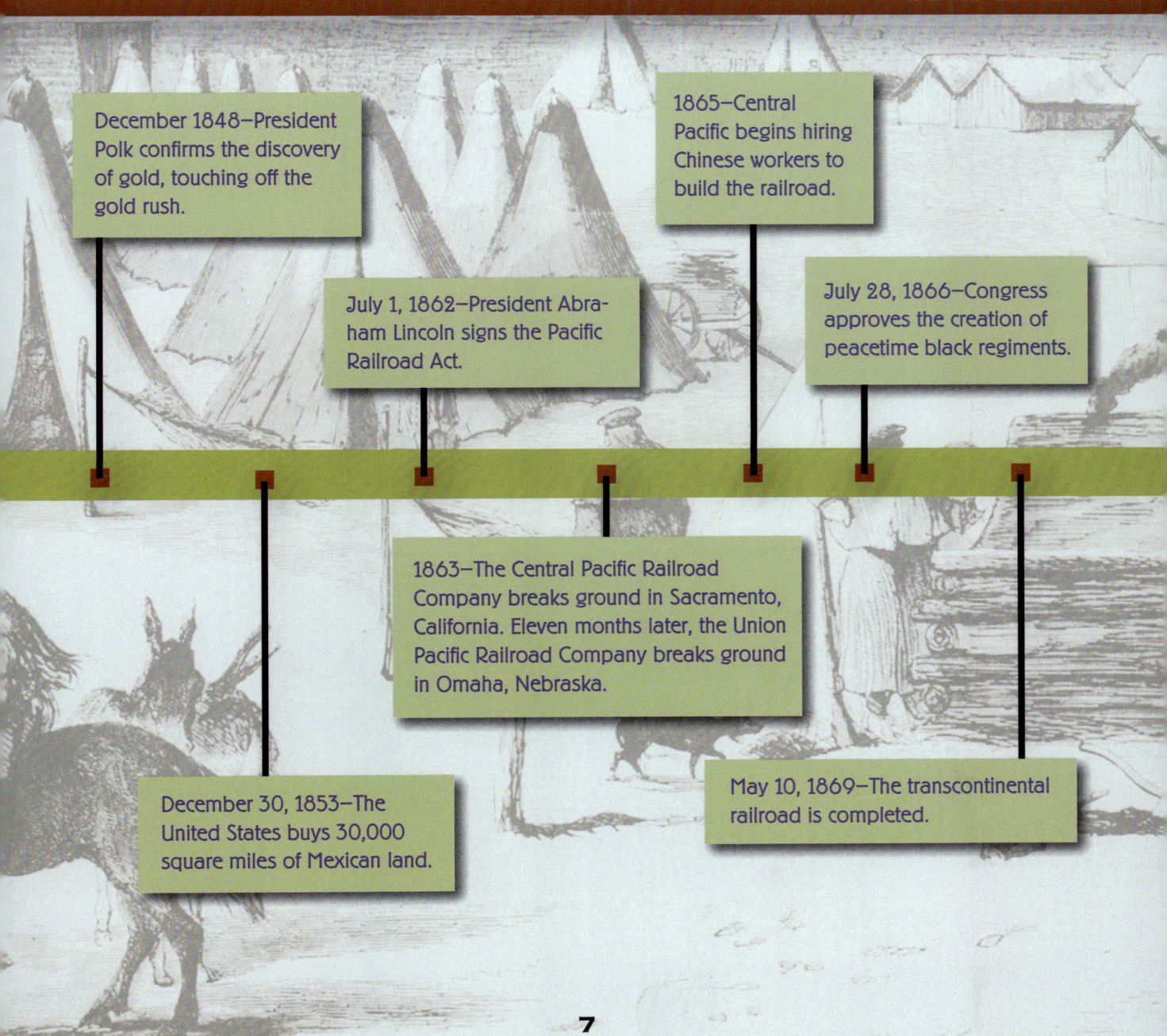

- **December 1848** – President Polk confirms the discovery of gold, touching off the gold rush.

- **December 30, 1853** – The United States buys 30,000 square miles of Mexican land.

- **July 1, 1862** – President Abraham Lincoln signs the Pacific Railroad Act.

- **1863** – The Central Pacific Railroad Company breaks ground in Sacramento, California. Eleven months later, the Union Pacific Railroad Company breaks ground in Omaha, Nebraska.

- **1865** – Central Pacific begins hiring Chinese workers to build the railroad.

- **July 28, 1866** – Congress approves the creation of peacetime black regiments.

- **May 10, 1869** – The transcontinental railroad is completed.

The Capitol Building, 1846

Chapter One
MANIFEST DESTINY

The American people wanted to move west. They were excited about making their country larger. Politicians and journalists wrote that Americans had the right to spread into the West. And not only did they have the right to move west, they also had the duty. Americans believed they were supposed to expand their country. They believed that was what God wanted them to do.

One journalist, named John O'Sullivan, wrote that the United States had a "Manifest Destiny" to spread out across North America. The word "manifest" means "obvious, or easy to see." The word "destiny" means "meant to happen." "Manifest Destiny" meant that the United States was clearly meant by God to spread out to the Pacific Ocean.

Americans loved the idea of Manifest Destiny. They believed the United States was the best country in the world. They believed everyone should be free. They thought everyone should help govern the country—as long as they were white and men, anyway. These freedoms were some of the **ideals** Americans believed. They believed God wanted them to spread these ideals. Spreading American beliefs was their job in life, they thought.

Ideals are things that people believe in. They are goals they work toward. Ideals are their picture of what life would be like if everything was perfect.

AMERICANS MOVE WEST

Manifest Destiny was a popular idea for another reason, too. The cities and towns in the East were getting crowded. A lot of Americans wanted space. Some people said that when you could see the smoke from your neighbor's chimney, it was time to move on. People wanted lots of room to themselves. They wanted to move west. Manifest Destiny made them feel moving west was the right thing to do.

During the 1844 presidential election, James Polk ran for president against Henry Clay. Polk wanted to **expand** the United States. He wanted Texas to become part of the country. He also thought the United States should claim the Oregon Territory. Clay, on the other hand, didn't want to think about expanding the country. He thought Americans should focus on other issues. People were excited about expansion, though. They believed in Manifest Destiny. Even though not everyone was sure Polk would make a good president, he was elected.

One big problem with Manifest Destiny was that the West wasn't empty. People lived there. Thousands of Native Americans already lived on the land. The United States had already forced thousands and thousands of eastern Native Americans to move west. They had pushed the Native people out of their lands in the East. They had sent the Natives across the Mississippi River. Now, Americans wanted the Western land, too.

James Polk

Expand means to makes something bigger.

Manifest Destiny

The modern borders of the United States reflect the belief in Manifest Destiny.

AMERICANS MOVE WEST

A lot of Americans argued that they were doing a good thing by moving west. Manifest Destiny meant God wanted them to spread out. So they were doing what they were supposed to do. They thought they were bringing good things to the Native Americans, too. They thought the Native people would be better off if they learned how to live the way Europeans lived.

Native Americans already had their own way of life, though. Their **civilization** was just different from the civilization Americans brought.

Some Americans thought the Native Americans should change to fit in with whites' way of doing things. If they didn't change, some people thought the Natives would become extinct. They would stop existing as a special kind of people and they would become just like white people. Some people thought that would be okay. They thought maybe Native people ought to becoming extinct. They didn't think about how the Native people might think of it.

Racism was a big part of Manifest Destiny. Racism is when one group of people thinks they are better than other groups. If the American settlers believed the Native Americans or the Mexicans were their equals, they wouldn't be able to say it was okay to push them off their land. Most Americans at the time thought white people were better than everyone else. They thought their ideas and religion were better, too. They believed white people needed to help non-white people. Sometimes, they thought helping them meant killing them or making them slaves. They didn't think about things from the other point of view.

Civilization is the way that a group of people live together, including their arts, their customs, their government, and their science.

Manifest Destiny

Not everybody agreed with Manifest Destiny, though. One politician, Charles Goodyear, said he hated hearing people talk about Manifest Destiny. He said he hated how Manifest Destiny had been used as an excuse for terrible violence and theft. Some other Americans felt the same way.

Some also disagreed with Manifest Destiny because of slavery. They thought slavery was wrong. They didn't like the idea of slavery spreading. They were afraid that if the United States grew, slavery would grow, too.

Most Americans did agree with Manifest Destiny, though. They thought it was a beautiful and good idea. They believed they were supposed to spread out into the West.

The Sioux watch farmers settling their lands.

AMERICANS MOVE WEST

Nineteenth-century Mexicans in California.

MANIFEST DESTINY

If Native Americans or Mexicans or anyone else tried to stop them, they believed they should fight.

And sometimes people did try to stop the Americans. When that happened, people fought each other. Sometimes it led to war.

An American Plains Indian

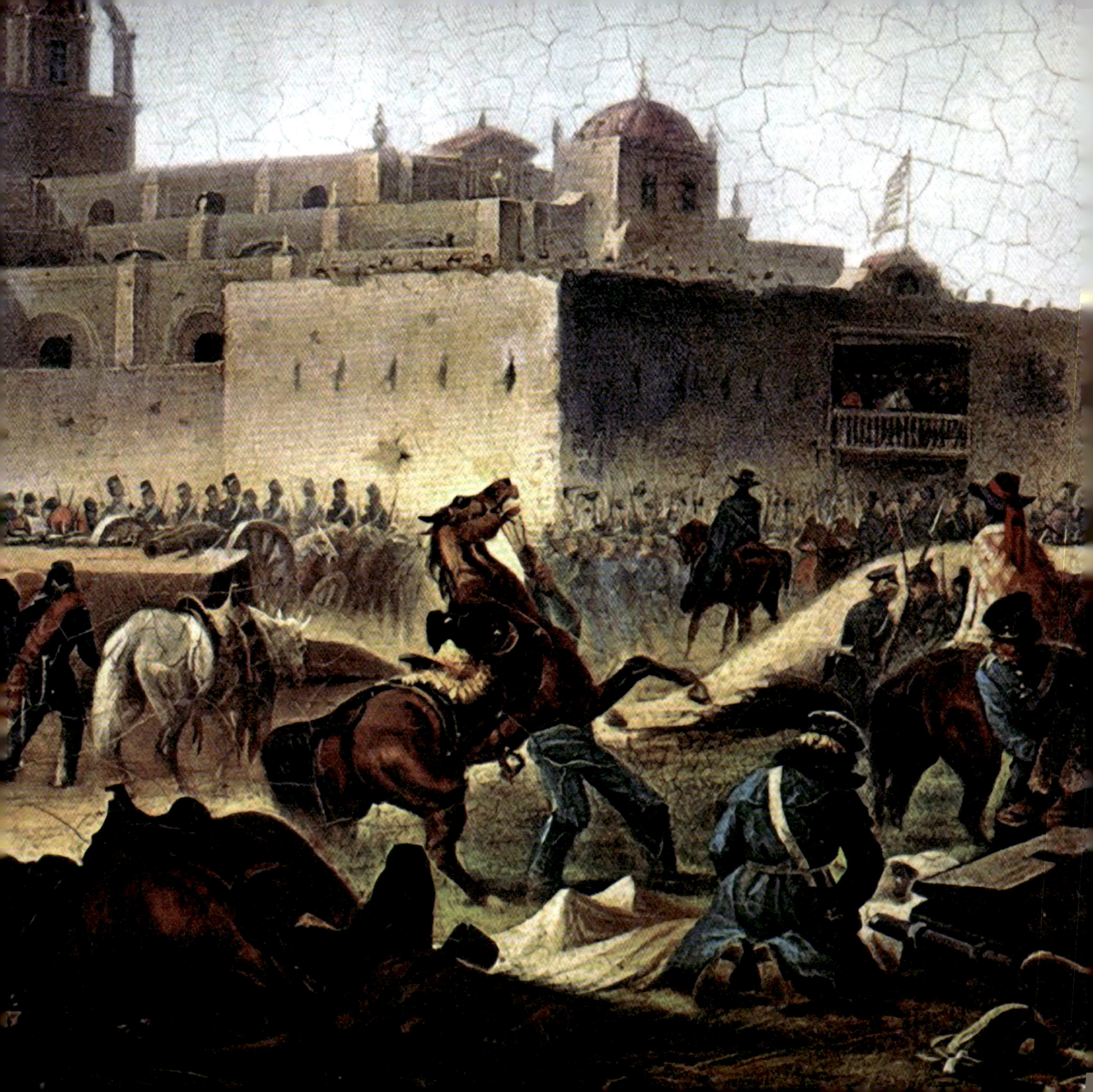

Chapter Two
WAR WITH MEXICO

On December 29, 1845, Texas became part of the United States. Mexico was not happy. The Americans said the border was the Rio Grande River. The Mexicans disagreed. They said the border was the Rio Nueces, over a hundred miles to the north.

The American president, James Polk, sent somebody to Mexico to talk about the problem. Polk didn't want to fight with Mexico. He wanted to solve the problem. The United States wanted to buy New Mexico and California. The man who Polk sent offered Mexico money for New Mexico, California, and the part of Texas between the Rio Nueces and the Rio Grande. Polk said the United States would pay the three million dollars that Mexico owed to American settlers in Texas. That would be the payment for the territory.

The Mexicans were insulted by the American offer. They didn't think they owed the American settlers anything. And they'd never given up their claim on Texas, either. They stopped doing business with the United States completely.

President Polk worried Mexico would start a war with the United States. He sent an army to patrol along the Rio Grande. General Zachary Taylor commanded the army.

AMERICANS MOVE WEST

On April 25, 1846, Colonel Seth Thornton was leading a group of seventy American soldiers. They were patrolling in Southeast Texas. The weather was very hot. They were looking for a place to rest and stay for the night. Their guide had told them about an empty hacienda—a large estate. When they saw it, they headed for it. They were ready to relax.

When they got to the hacienda, though, they found it wasn't empty at all. Instead, two thousand Mexican soldiers were inside. Nobody knows exactly what happened next. Someone fired a shot. Fighting broke out. For hours, the fighting raged. Sixteen American soldiers were killed. Finally, the Mexican soldiers captured the rest of the Americans. They took them prisoner and brought them back to Mexico. The conflict became known as the Thornton Affair.

President Polk was upset when he heard about the Thornton Affair. He went to Congress and asked it to declare war on Mexico. On May 13, Congress officially declared war.

Not all Americans were happy about the war. People in the Northern states were especially unhappy. They were afraid the war meant the South was trying to get more slave states.

The Mexican War took place in several areas. Colonel Stephen Kearny led part of the army toward Santa Fe, New Mexico. He didn't want to fight a long and terrible battle. So he sent two men on ahead to meet with the Mexican general in Santa Fe. When Kearny and his troops got to Santa Fe, the Mexican soldiers had gone. He wasn't sure what had happened. He never knew for sure, but he wondered if the men he had sent had bribed the Mexican general to leave. Whatever had happened, Kearny was able to take the city without having to fight at all.

Kearny got people together to govern Santa Fe. Then he took his men and set out for California. On the way, they met Kit Carson riding east. Carson, a trapper and scout,

WAR WITH MEXICO

was bringing news. In Sonoma, California, American settlers hadn't wanted to wait for the U.S. Army to arrive. They had gone to the Mexican general, Mariano Vallejo, and demanded he surrender. Vallejo said he would rather California be ruled by the United States than Mexico. He asked if he could join the Americans. The Americans weren't sure about this, so they took him prisoner. Later, though, Vallejo would go on to become a California state senator.

The Americans in Sonoma made a flag and raised it. The flag had a star, a stripe, a grizzly bear, and the words "California Republic." What happened became known as the Bear Flag Revolt.

When Kearny heard about the Bear Flag Revolt, he relaxed. He sent most of his men back to Santa Fe. Then he, Kit Carson, and a hundred men rode toward San Diego. Before they got to California, though, they started hearing rumors about trouble. The Californios—the Spanish-speaking people in California who had come originally from Mexico or Spain—were not happy about becoming part of the United States.

Kearny and his men were very tired. They had been traveling for several months. When they reached the village of San Pasqual, just outside San Diego, they met a large army of Californios. They were tired and outnumbered, but they fought anyway. Over

AMERICANS MOVE WEST

Colonel Stephen Kearny

WAR WITH MEXICO

WHAT'S A PARALLEL?

The 49th parallel was a circle of latitude. Latitude is made up of imaginary circles drawn on the Earth's globe. They help measure the distance between the poles and the equator.

one-third of their men were killed or injured. Eventually, American soldiers from San Diego arrived. Kearny and his men were able to pull back from the battle. They went to San Diego and got organized.

On January 13, 1847, Kearny and the Americans were able to finally end the Californio rebellion. On that day, the Mexican governor in California, Andrés Pico, signed the Treaty of Cahuenga. The treaty wasn't official. It was just an agreement between the two sides to stop fighting. Later, when the war ended, the Californios would become citizens of the United States.

Kearny fought the Mexican-American War in New Mexico and California. General Winfield Scott, meanwhile, was marching toward Mexico City. The American troops led by Scott reached the edge of the city in September 1847. Over the next week, they fought several battles with the Mexican troops. Finally, the Americans captured the city.

On February 2, 1848, Mexico and the United States signed the Treaty of Guadalupe Hidalgo. The treaty ended the war. In the treaty, Mexico also agreed to sell one-third of

AMERICANS MOVE WEST

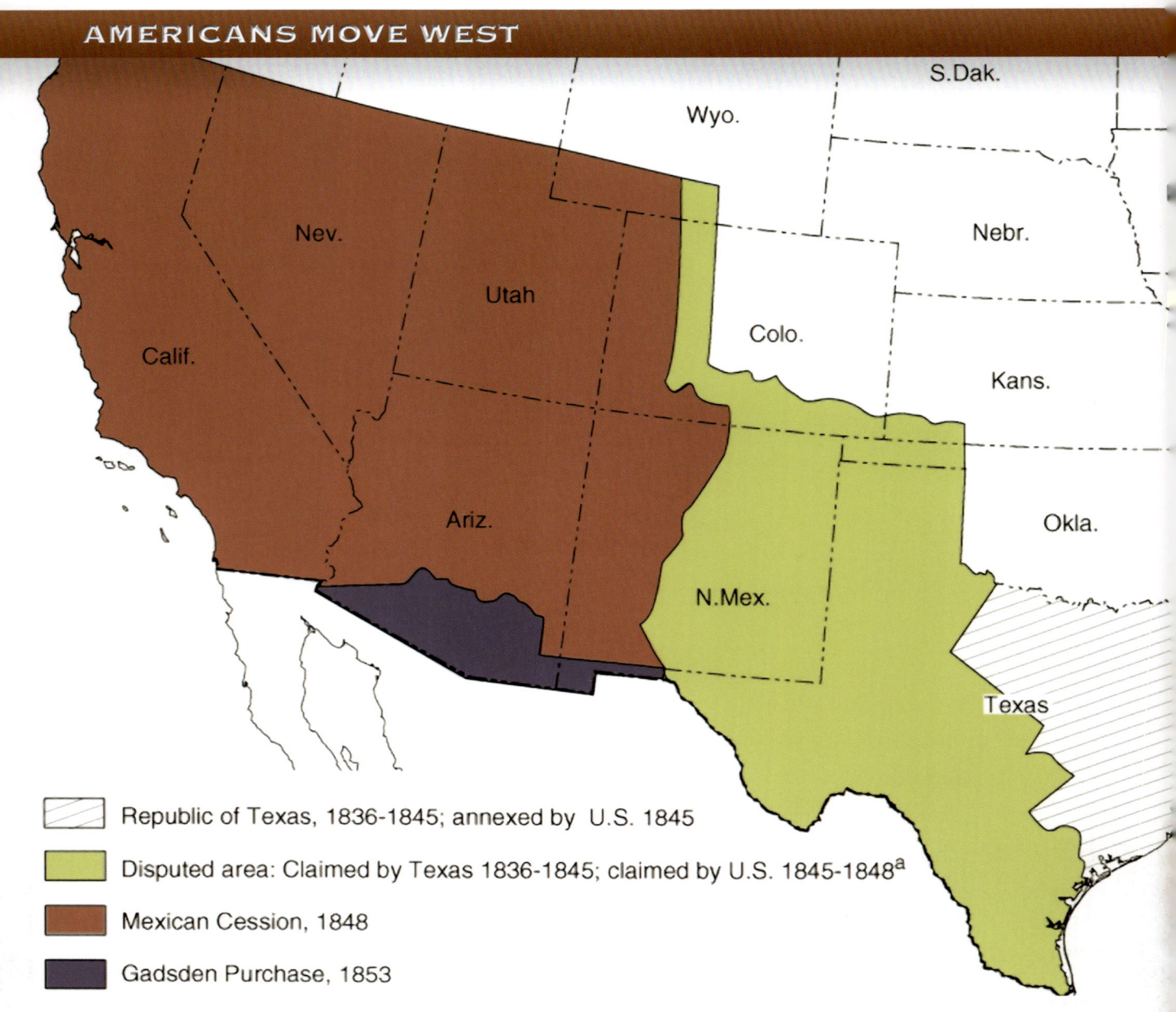

- Republic of Texas, 1836-1845; annexed by U.S. 1845
- Disputed area: Claimed by Texas 1836-1845; claimed by U.S. 1845-1848[a]
- Mexican Cession, 1848
- Gadsden Purchase, 1853

Map of land gained from Mexico.

War with Mexico

its territory to the United States. This land was called the Mexican Cession. It included California, Nevada, and Utah. It also included parts of Arizona, New Mexico, Colorado, and Wyoming. The United States would pay $15 million for the area.

As the Mexican-American War was going on, Americans were thinking about the Oregon Territory, too. At first, President Polk had wanted to claim all of Oregon Territory. That would have given the United States a huge piece of land reaching north to the Southern border of Alaska. Finally, on June 15, 1846, the United States and Britain signed the Oregon Treaty. The treaty set the border between the United States and Britain at the 49th parallel, which is where it is today.

The occupation of Mexico's capital by the American Army.

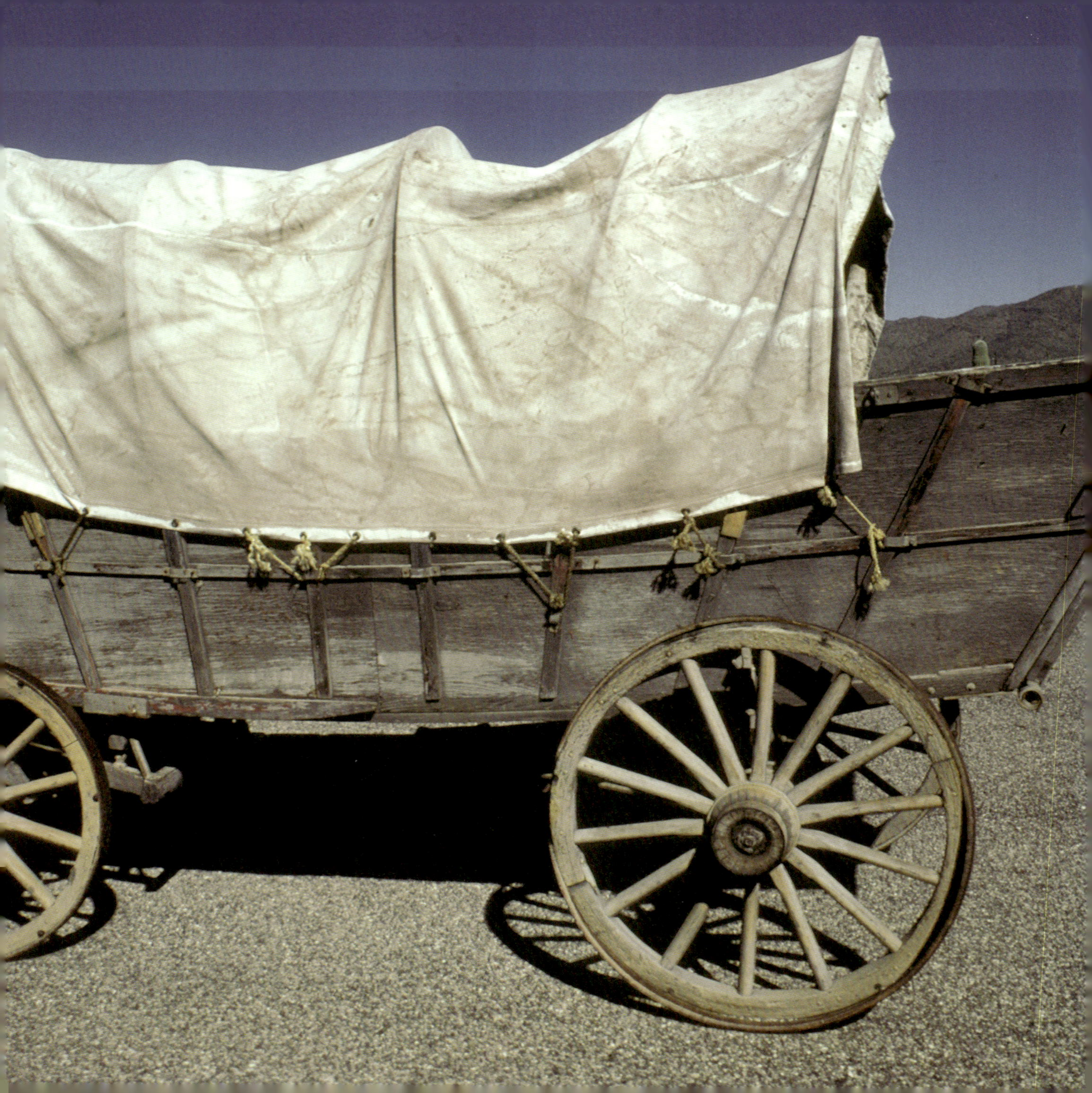

Chapter Three
WHY PEOPLE MOVED WEST

In the United States in the 1800s, moving west was a big deal. You had to leave your friends and family behind. You had to leave behind the life you were used to. If you lived in a town in the Eastern United States, you would have stores nearby. You would have neighbors. You would have a school not far away. But life in the West was very different. It could be very hard.

LAND

People who moved west packed everything they owned into a wagon and set off across the country. They had to cross thousands of miles of wilderness. Just crossing a river was hard! People died from hunger or sickness. Sometimes they were killed by Native Americans. About one out of every ten settlers died on the trip west.

Manifest Destiny wasn't the reason people moved west. They wanted to move west. Manifest Destiny just helped them explain why they should move west.

One of the main reasons people moved west was because they wanted land. Farmers in the East felt crowded. Children from farm families grew up and wanted their own farms. But they couldn't always find enough land nearby. In the West, there was lots of land.

Newspapers wrote about all the land in the West. They drew pictures of happy pioneer families. They didn't talk about the dangers very much, though.

RELIGION

Land was just one reason people moved west. Another reason was religious freedom. The Mormon Church had started in Western New York in 1830. Joseph Smith started the church. He said an angel named Moroni told him where to find a special book. Smith called the book The Book of Mormon. Smith told people about the book. Gradually, people started to listen to him. Together, they formed the Mormon Church. This is also called the Church of Jesus Christ of Latter-day Saints.

Some people really didn't like the Mormons. They didn't like the things Joseph Smith was teaching. He said that a Hebrew family had traveled from Israel to South America in thousands of years ago. He also said that all the Native Americans had descended from this family.

Other people didn't like the Mormons because their group grew quickly. They did business with other Mormons before they did business with non-Mormons. Some people thought they might hurt American's businesses. They also thought they might be take away America's religious beliefs.

Sometimes, people who didn't like the Mormons destroyed their things. Sometimes, they threatened to hurt the Mormons. Because of this, Smith and the Mormons moved from Western New York to Ohio in 1831.

The Mormons had trouble in Ohio, too, though. Their church kept growing. But so did the number of people who didn't like them. Over the next fifteen years, the Mormons

Why People Moved West

Joseph Smith and the handwritten account of his vision.

AMERICANS MOVE WEST

moved from Ohio to Missouri to Illinois, and finally to Utah. During that time, Joseph Smith was killed by people who didn't like the Mormons. Brigham Young took over leading the church.

The Mormons traveled west to Salt Lake City, Utah. They built the Mormon Pioneer Trail. Along the trail, they set up places for travelers to stay. They built ferries to make it easier to cross rivers.

Mormons traveling to Utah.

GOLD

In 1848, people found yet another reason to move west. A man named James Marshall was building a sawmill next to the American River in Northern California. Suddenly, he noticed something sparkling in the water. It was gold!

Marshall's boss, John Sutter, owned the land. He didn't want people coming to his land to look for gold. Marshall and Sutter agreed to keep the gold a secret.

Sutter had built a town called Sutter's Fort nearby, though. People in Sutter's Fort started hearing rumors about the gold. A secret about gold was hard to keep.

One man, Sam Brannan, owned a store in Sutter's Fort. Without telling anyone, he bought all the pick axes, pans, and shovels he could find in Northern California. Then he collected a bottle of gold dust from the river.

WHY PEOPLE MOVED WEST

Brannan traveled eighty-five miles to San Francisco, which was then called Yerba Buena. He stood in the street and held up the bottle of gold dust. "Gold!" he yelled. "Gold on the American River!"

Soon, excitement had spread through the city. Everyone wanted to be rich!

Brannan had known what he was doing. Anyone who wanted to look for gold would need equipment. And Brannan had bought all the equipment. Everyone had to buy it from him. He made everything very expensive. A pan might have cost 15 cents a few days before. Now, Brannan was selling it for $8. In just a few weeks, Brannan made $36,000! (And today, this would be millions of dollars!)

Gold prospectors in California.

AMERICANS MOVE WEST

News of the gold took a while to spread across the country. People in the East heard rumors about the gold. They weren't sure if they believed the stories, though. Then, in December 1848, President Polk gave the State of the Union Address. In it, he talked about the gold that had been discovered in California. He said a huge amount of gold had been found.

Polk's speech convinced Americans the gold was real. Thousands of men left their families and raced across the country toward California. They wanted to get there quickly, get rich, and then go home.

For most people, this plan didn't work at all. For one thing, getting across the country was very hard. Many died along the trails. They got sick. They drowned in rivers. Some were killed in accidents. Some people turned around and went home. The gold wasn't worth the trip for them.

The number of white settlers in California jumped from 13,000 to 300,000 between 1848 and 1854. Very few of them got rich. So many people had come looking for gold that most could barely earn enough money to pay for food and supplies. Some changed their plans and decided to open a store or laundry or barbershop instead. These people sometimes ended up a lot richer than the miners.

Americans weren't the only people who rushed to California to find gold. People came from all over the world to get rich. The American miners weren't always happy about these people. There wasn't as much gold as people had thought. California passed a Foreign Miners Tax. Miners who had come from other countries now had to pay $20 a month in order to look for gold. A lot of them gave up and went home. The gold wasn't worth the problems. Especially because gold had become hard to find.

The Chinese were one group that succeeded in California. Instead of giving up and going home, the Chinese banded together. They helped each other. They built China-

Why People Moved West

towns. These Chinatowns were like a little piece of home for the Chinese. Many men had left their families behind. They helped each other in their new country.

Many Americans didn't like the Chinese, though. The Chinese were willing to work hard and do jobs no one else wanted. They would sometimes take an abandoned mine and find gold in it. Other miners had thought the mine had no more gold. But the Chinese found gold that was hard to get out.

California made the Chinese pay extra taxes. They had to pay the Foreign Miners Tax and another tax that was just for the Chinese. But they didn't get discouraged and leave. Instead, most of them stayed and made a life for themselves. Over the next hundred and fifty years, American accepted the Chinese and came to respect them.

The gold rush changed California in a lot of ways. Hundreds of thousands of people came to the area. Native Americans got crowded off of their land. Forests were cut down. Streams were filled in. The miners used mercury to get the gold out of the rock. The poisonous mercury killed fish and animals. It killed many miners too. The mercury stayed in the land, too. It will stay in the rivers and dirt for thousands of years.

The Mormon pioneers, the gold rush, and the wish for more land brought people to the Western United States. And these settlers changed the United States forever.

A Chinese miner.

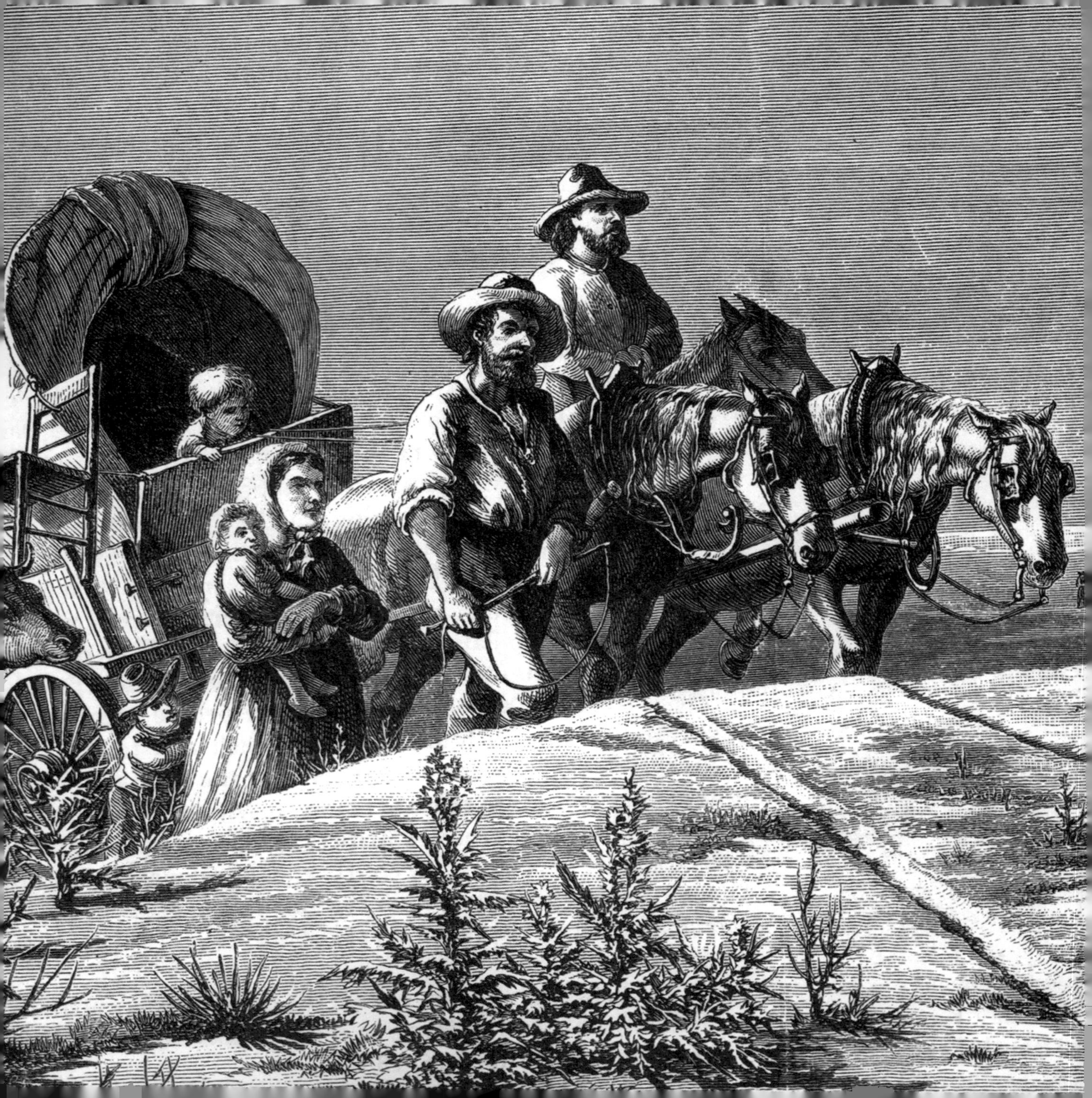

Chapter Four
LIFE ON THE OREGON TRAIL

In April 1846, Mary Munkers and her family left Missouri. They were heading out on the Oregon Trail. She and her parents, her seven brothers and sisters, and the families of her three married brothers and sisters put everything they owned into covered wagons. For day after day, their wagons rolled across the prairie.

One night, a storm blew up. Mary and her family huddled in their tents. Thunder growled. Lightning flashed. Drenching rain started to pour down. Suddenly, a wild wind pulled the tents open. Everyone was soaking wet! The men quickly ran from wagon to wagon. They tied them together to keep them from blowing over into the river. They tied the tents back down. All night the storm raged. Mary and the others tried to sleep. In the morning, the storm had ended. The family checked to see what damage the storm had done. The wagons had survived, but their things had been blown all over the place. Mary and the family spent most of the morning gathering their belongings. Some things would be okay. Some were completely ruined.

The Munkers family was lucky. The storm was one of the worst things that happened to them on their way to Oregon. Many people weren't so lucky.

AMERICANS MOVE WEST

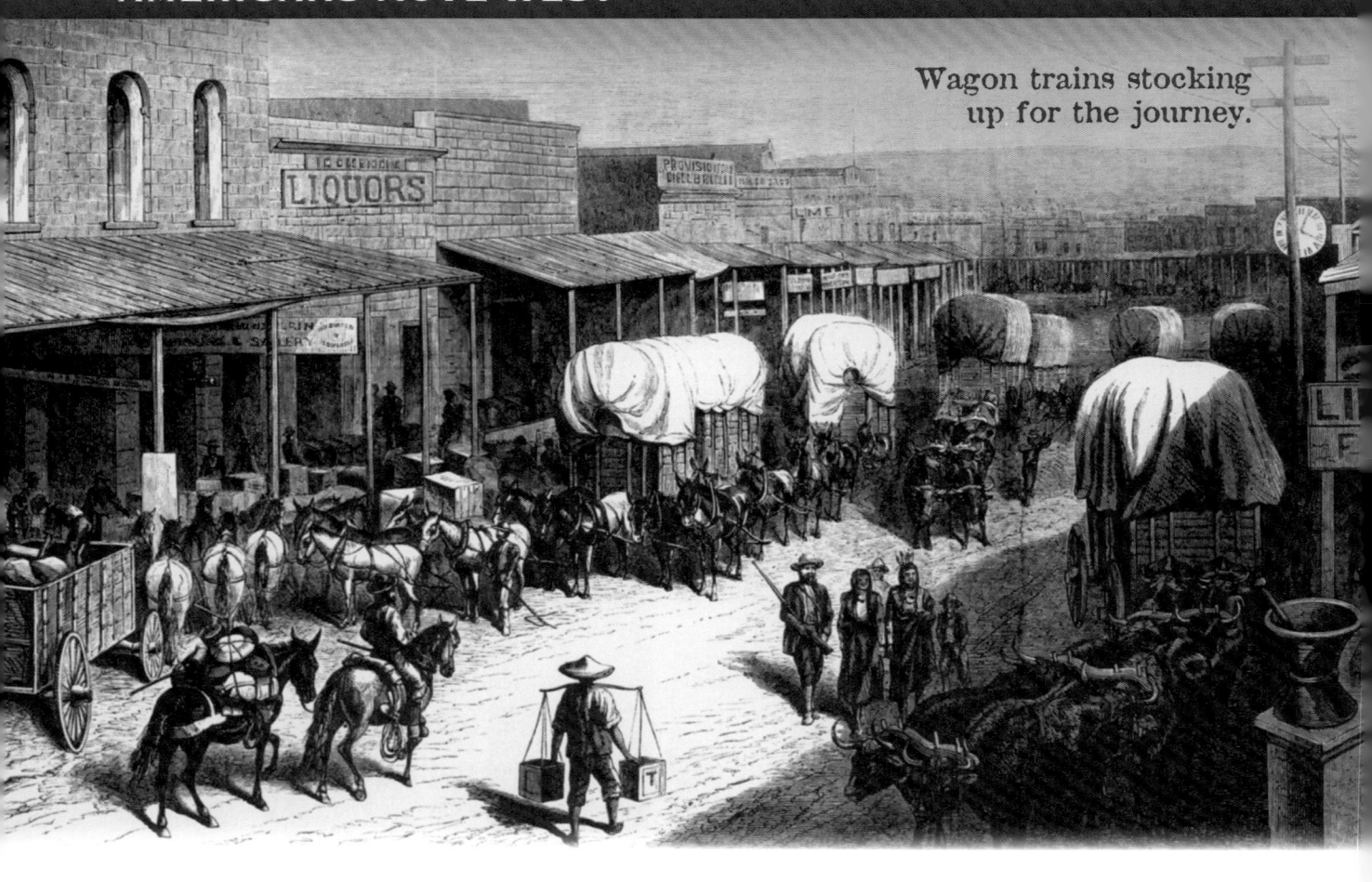

Wagon trains stocking up for the journey.

The Oregon Trail was a popular route to the West. Between about 1843 and 1869, thousands of people loaded their belongings into wagons and set out across the country.

A trip across the Oregon Trail took about five or six months. The really lucky people could make it in four months. When people ran into trouble, though, the trip could take even longer. A longer trip caused problems. A longer trip meant people had to deal with winter weather. It also meant they had to bring more food and supplies.

LIFE ON THE OREGON TRAIL

The beginning of the Oregon Trail was in Independence, Missouri. Sometimes people joined the trail further along to the west, though. Each winter and spring, people came to Independence. They bought supplies and got ready. They tried to bring everything they might need on the way. Most people bought oxen to pull the wagons. Oxen could pull a heavier load than horses. They were also cheaper.

Then, in late April or early May, it was time to leave. Everyone tried to get in line. Wagons got tangled together. Some people had never driven a wagon before. Driving a wagon could be tricky. Some people had trouble steering the oxen. Some even tipped over their wagons. All their things spilled out on the ground. They had to get the wagon back upright and reloaded.

Many times, as soon as people started out, they realized they had packed too much. The oxen had trouble pulling the heavy load. Most people walked instead of riding. Then the oxen wouldn't have to pull them, too. But, even then, the oxen got tired quickly. The heaviest wagons fell behind the others. Just outside Independence, people who had packed too much started throwing things away. For a few miles, the trail would be lined with furniture, crates, and piles of food. People went through their wagons and dumped whatever they thought they could live without.

Before setting out on the Oregon Trail, a lot of people worried about being attacked by Native Americans. Really, though, attacks like this were

Native Americans were not as dangerous to settlers as many of the settlers thought.

AMERICANS MOVE WEST

very rare. Native Americans were more likely to silently watch the wagons go by. Sometimes Native Americans rode into the pioneers' camps to trade. At other times, they helped pioneers whose wagons had gotten stuck in mud or swept away by a river.

The real dangers on the Oregon Trail were diseases, accidents—and getting worn out from walking so far. The worst disease was cholera. Cholera was spread by dirty water or food. People didn't understand that then. They didn't know why people got cholera. They only knew that sometimes people would be healthy in the morning and dead by night. They would suddenly get stomach cramps. They would throw up and get diarrhea. People who died were quickly buried along the side of the trail.

A pioneer family.

LIFE ON THE OREGON TRAIL

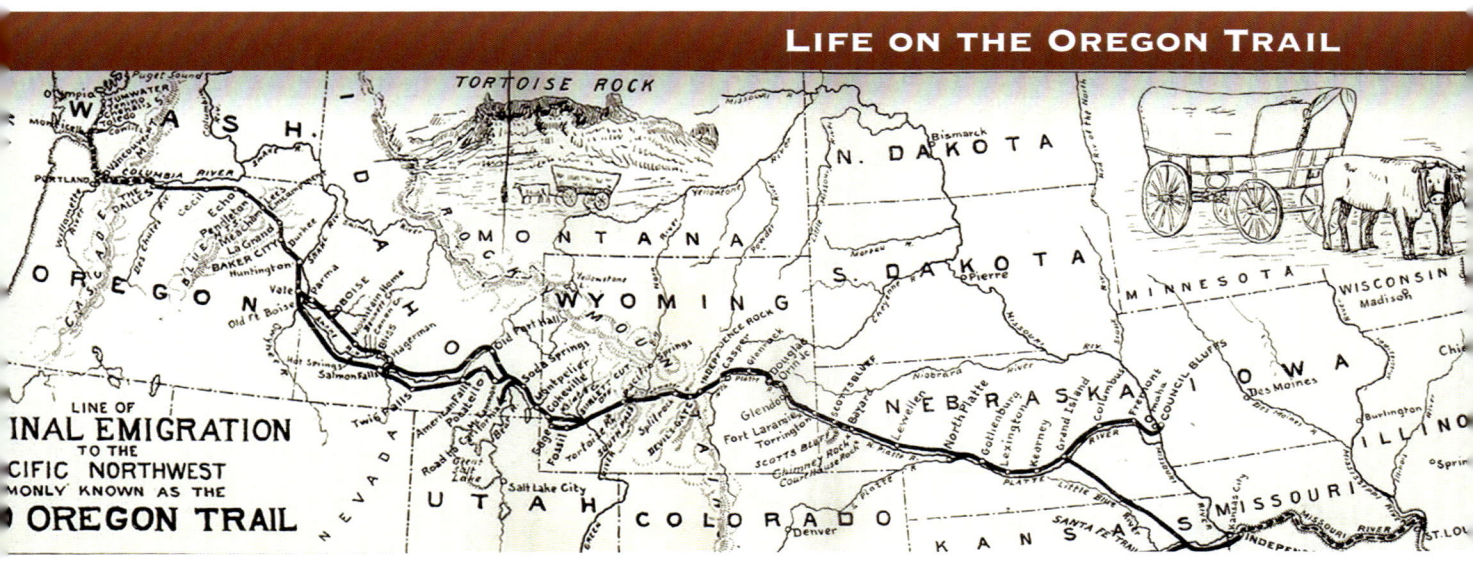

Map of the Oregon Trail.

Accidents killed a lot of people on the Oregon Trail, too. The most common accident was being accidentally shot with a gun.

River crossings were also very dangerous. Sometimes wagons were swept away when people tried to cross a stream or river. Deeper rivers often had ferries. These ferries were like large flat rafts. Usually, the ferrymen took the wagons across one at a time. Sometimes ferrymen tried to overload the ferries. This could be very dangerous. The ferries sometimes tipped over. The ferries were also very expensive. Since everyone had to cross the river, the ferrymen could charge whatever they wanted.

Exhaustion was a problem for everyone, both people and animals. Most people walked, so the wagon would be lighter for the oxen. But wagons were still very heavy. Sometimes they were so heavy the oxen died from exhaustion.

For years, the Oregon Trail was a big part of the United States. Thousands of people followed the route west. Then, on May 10, 1869, the last spike was pounded into the cross-country railroad. Suddenly, people had a faster, cheaper, and safer way to travel. The days of the Oregon Trail were over.

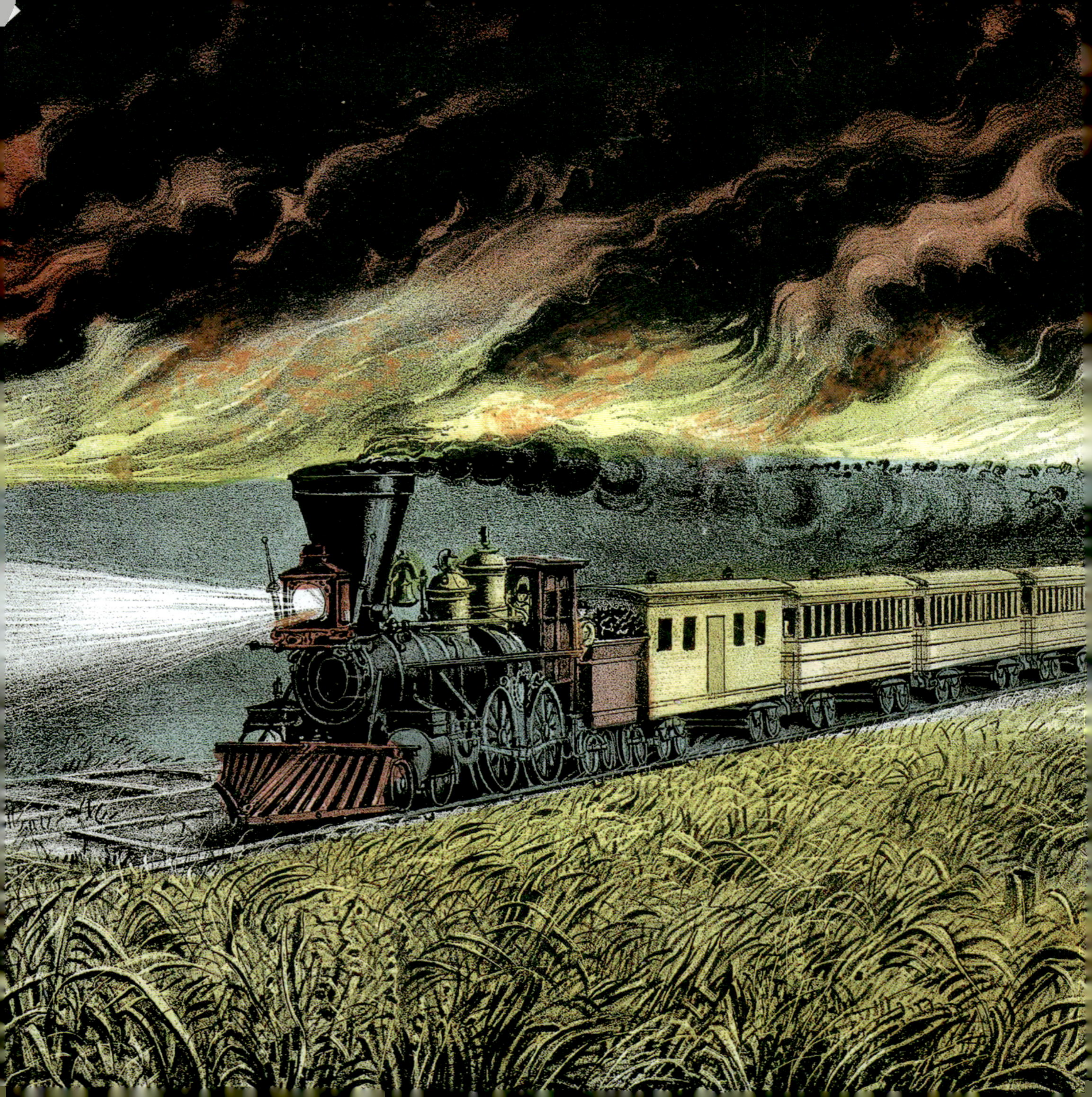

Chapter Five
A RAILROAD ACROSS THE UNITED STATES

On May 10, 1869, a crowd of people gathered at Promontory Point. This was a little valley in Utah. They had come to watch the last spike of the railroad be hammered in. Reporters waited. Photographers set up their cameras. The president of the Central Pacific Railroad Company, Leland Stanford, picked up a golden spike. The spike had been made especially for this moment. At 2:47 in the afternoon, Stanford pounded the spike into the railroad. It was done! The railroad stretching across the country was finally finished.

Settlers had been traveling across the United States for years. People had been talking about building a railroad across the country ever since locomotives had been invented in the early 1800s. At first, a lot of people worried that railroads would be too dangerous. The first trains went about fifteen miles an hour. This was a lot faster than people were used to. Many people were too terrified to ride on the new vehicle.

Railroads became more common, though. People got used to them. Small, unconnected railroads were built in parts of the East. People kept talking about connecting the railroads and building a railroad line across the country.

AMERICANS MOVE WEST

Building the railroad.

A Railroad Across the United States

The idea of a railroad line connecting the different parts of the country slowly became more popular. But Americans disagreed about where the railroad should be built. There were three ideas.

Many in the North thought the railroad should start in Chicago, Illinois. This would mean it was closer to New York and Boston. These were two of the American cities with the most people living in them.

People in the South thought the railroad should start in Memphis, Tennessee. The South had a lot of big farms. But it didn't have very many factories. Southerners thought building the railroad across the South would help bring in more jobs and money. People in the North didn't like the idea of building the railroad in the South, though. They thought it would spread slavery further across the country.

The third idea was to start the railroad in St. Louis, Missouri. This would be a middle option, between the other two ideas. People in St. Louis thought building the railroad there made sense. The Oregon Trail already started in Missouri. It seemed only right to start the railroad there, as well.

The government thought hard about all the ideas. The leaders wanted to make a good choice. Finally, they decided to go with the central route. But instead of starting in Missouri, the railroad would start in Omaha, Nebraska. The Civil War was raging in the East. A lot of fighting was happening in Missouri.

On July 1, 1862, President Abraham Lincoln signed the Pacific Railroad Act. The act said the Union Pacific Railroad would start building in Omaha. At the same time, the Central Pacific Railroad would start building in Sacramento, California. The two railroads would build toward each other. Then they would meet in the middle.

In Sacramento, work started on January 8, 1863. At the end of that year, work started in Omaha. Six years later, the two ends would meet.

AMERICANS MOVE WEST

Finding workers to build the railroad turned out to be difficult. The work was very hard. The conditions were miserable. Working on the railroad could also be very dangerous. In 1865, the Central Pacific Railroad tried to hire 5,000 men. Nowhere near this many asked for the job, though. Of those who did come, 90 percent quit after a week. The work was too hard.

THE RAILROAD AND CHINESE AMERICANS

After a while, someone suggested the railroad hire Chinese **immigrants**. The company wasn't sure that was a good idea. Most of the Chinese men were less than five feet tall. They didn't look strong enough to do the difficult work. Still, the railroad needed workers. So the company agreed to hire fifty Chinese men. The bosses were surprised when the Chinese worked harder and better than anyone else. They did the work well. They didn't complain. Quickly, the railroads hired thousands more Chinese immigrants.

The cross-country railroad made settling the West much easier. But it caused problems, too.

THE RAILROAD AND NATIVE AMERICANS

The Native Americans had been pushed further and further west. Now there was nowhere else for them to go. Their homelands had been overrun with settlers. They had used the huge herds of bison on the plains for their food. The bison had been a big part of the way

Immigrants are people who leave their home countries to move to another country to live.

A Railroad Across the United States

AMERICANS MOVE WEST

The completion of the transcontinental railroad at Promontory Point, Utah.

A Railroad Across the United States

they lived their lives. But the railroad companies had killed thousands of these bison. The herds had become very small.

The Americans and the Native Americans did not often live together well. The Americans forced the Native Americans to leave whenever they wanted their land. If they wanted it quickly, they sometimes killed the Native Americans who lived there.

By the end of the 1800s, most Native Americans lived on reservations. These reservations were small pieces of land set aside for them. The Native Americans couldn't move across the land as they once had. Once, they had had lots of freedom and space. They had had exactly what the American pioneers wanted. Now, their lives had been changed forever.

DIFFERENT STORIES

The story of American expansion into the West has good parts and bad. The stories of the pioneers are stories of brave people facing hardships. But the effect on the land and on the Native Americans makes the stories sad.

Americans had great ideas about the world. They thought everyone should be free and able to decide their own lives. But these ideas didn't always work out. And there were always some people who had to give up their freedoms so that Americans could have theirs. Their stories got in each other's way.

FIND OUT MORE

In Books

Hermes, Patricia. *Westward to Home: Joshua's Oregon Trail Diary.* New York: Scholastic, 2002.

King, David C. *Westward Expansion.* Hoboken, N.J.: Wiley, 2003.

Olson, Nathan. *The Building of the Transcontinental Railroad.* Mankato, Minn.: Capstone, 2007.

On the Internet

The Oregon Trail: 1843 Map
www.historyglobe.com/ot/otmap1.htm

The Oregon Trail: The Game
www.oregontrail.com

Transcontinental Railroad
www.pbs.org/wgbh/amex/tcrr/

Westward Movement
www.socialstudiesforkids.com/subjects/westwardmovement.htm

INDEX

Bear Flag Revolt 19

Carson, Kit 18, 19
Central Pacific Railroad 39, 41, 42
Chinese 30, 31, 42
civilization 12
Clay, Henry 10

Goodyear, Charles 13

immigrants 42

Kearny, Stephen 18–21

Lincoln, Abraham 14

Manifest Destiny 9–15, 25
Marshall, James 28
Mexican-American War 21, 23
Mexicans 7, 12, 14, 17–19, 21, 23
Mormon 26. 28, 31

Mormon Pioneer Trail 28

Native Americans 10, 12, 15, 25, 26, 31, 35, 36, 42, 45

Oregon Trail 33–37, 41
O'Sullivan, John 9

Polk, James 10, 17, 18, 23, 30

racism 12

slavery 13, 41
Smith, Joseph 26–28
Sutter's Fort 28

Taylor, Zachary 17
Thornton, Seth 18
Treaty of Guadalupe Hidalgo 21

Vallejo, Mariano 19

ABOUT THE AUTHOR AND THE CONSULTANT

Teresa LaClair is an author who lives in New York State, but she was born in Canada. She has also written other books for kids.

Dr. Jack N. Rakove is a professor of history and American studies at Stanford University, where he is director of American studies. The winner of the 1997 Pulitzer Prize in history, Dr. Rakove is the author of *The Unfinished Election of 2000, Constitutional Culture and Democratic Rule*, and *James Madison and the Creation of the American Republic*. He is also the president of the Society for the History of the Early American Republic.

PICTURE CREDITS
Dover: p. 1, 6–7, 13, 29, 31, 32, 34, 35, 40, 43, 44
Makaristos: p. 19
Map Resources: p. 11
Monedula: p. 10
National Archives and Records Administration: p. 8, 36
Pearson Scott Foresman: p. 21
Photos.com: p. 15, 24, 38
U.S. National Park Service: p. 23
University of California: p. 14
University of Texas: p. 37
Y.B. Welch: p. 20

To the best knowledge of the publisher, all other images are in the public domain. If any image has been inadvertently uncredited, please notify Harding House Publishing Services, Vestal, New York 13850, so that rectification can be made for future printings.